GETTING STARTED WITH EXCEL
FOR TOM'S WEAR

Executive editor: Deborah Hoffman
Managing editor: Alana Bradley
Production editor: Carol Zaino
Manufacturer: Integrated Book Technology

ISBN 0-13-047303-0

10

GETTING STARTED WITH EXCEL FOR TOM'S WEAR

Patti Lopez
Valencia Community College

Pearson
Education

Upper Saddle River, New Jersey 07458

TABLE OF CONTENTS

Excel Workshop

CHAPTER 1

Creating a Simple Spreadsheet for Tom's Wear, Inc., Using the Accounting Equation

Before beginning this assignment, read Parts A & B of the Computerized Accounting appendix at the back of this book.

How to open Excel

1. Click on the Start button. Point to Programs: select Microsoft Excel. Your desktop may have an Excel icon that allows you to enter the program by double-clicking it.

2. Follow the instructions in Part A of the Computerized Accounting appendix at the back of this book to open a new Excel workbook.

How to create bold headings

3. Create the following bold column headings beginning in Cell A1 and ending in Column J: **Date, Description, Cash +, Other Assets =** (*two column heading*), **Liabilities +** (*two column heading*), **Contributed Capital +, Retained Earnings** (*two column heading*). To bold text highlight the cells containing the text and click the **Bold** button **B** .

How to change text alignment

4. Wrap the "Contributed Capital" text by selecting cell H1 and then choosing **Format, Cells, Alignment** from the menu bar. Click on the **"Wrap text"** box.

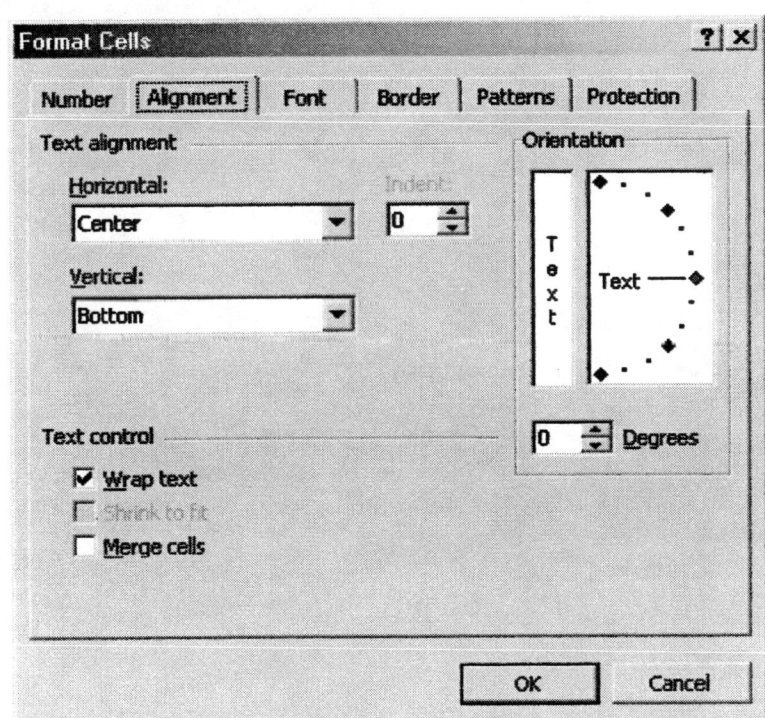

How to adjust column widths

Adjust the column widths as needed using one of the following methods:

- Holding down your left mouse button and drag when you see the arrow depicted below:

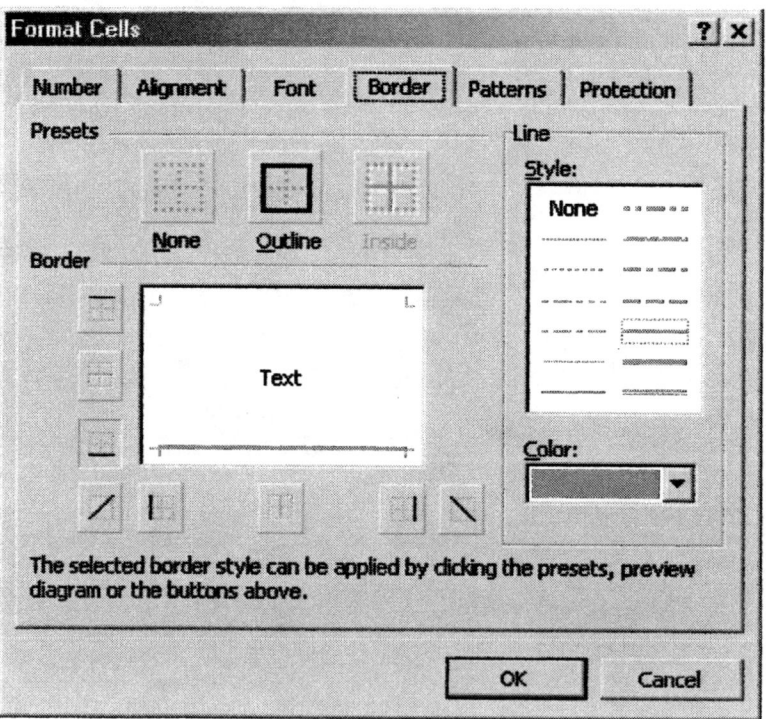

- Double click your left mouse button when you see the arrow depicted above. Double clicking will automatically resize your column based on the longest line.

How to center text

5. Highlight both cells and click the **Merge and Center** button 🔲 to center your two-column headings across both columns. Highlight all your headings and click the **Center** button 📄 to center all column headings.

How to underline headings

6. Underline your heading by selecting **Format, Cells, Border** from the menu bar

7. Once these steps are completed, your screen should look like this:

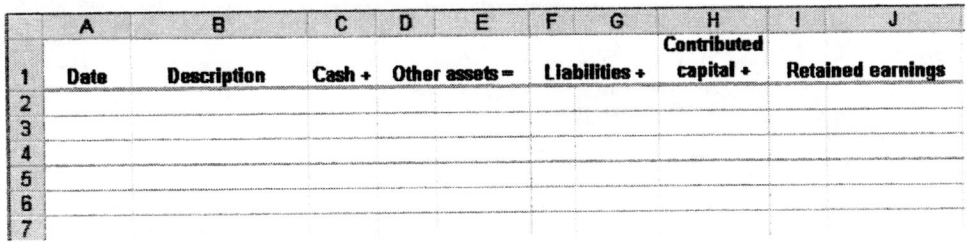

	A	B	C	D	E	F	G	H	I	J
1	Date	Description	Cash +	Other assets =		Liabilities +		Contributed capital +	Retained earnings	
2										
3										
4										
5										
6										
7										

8. Tom's Wear, Inc. is a wholesale company that sells t-shirts. Input the following transactions from the month of February into your spreadsheet. Adjust your column widths and use "Wrap text" as needed.

2/01/2001   Tom invested an additional $2,000 in the company.
2/03/2001   Tom bought 300 shirts for $4 each and paid cash.
2/05/2001   Tom sold 100 shirts for $10 each.
2/25/2001   Tom paid his $30 telephone bill for February telephone service.
2/28/2001   Tom purchased a piece of equipment on credit for $600.

How to format numbers

9. Format your numbers by selecting **Format, Cells, Number**. Highlight the cells to be formatted and use the currency format as shown:

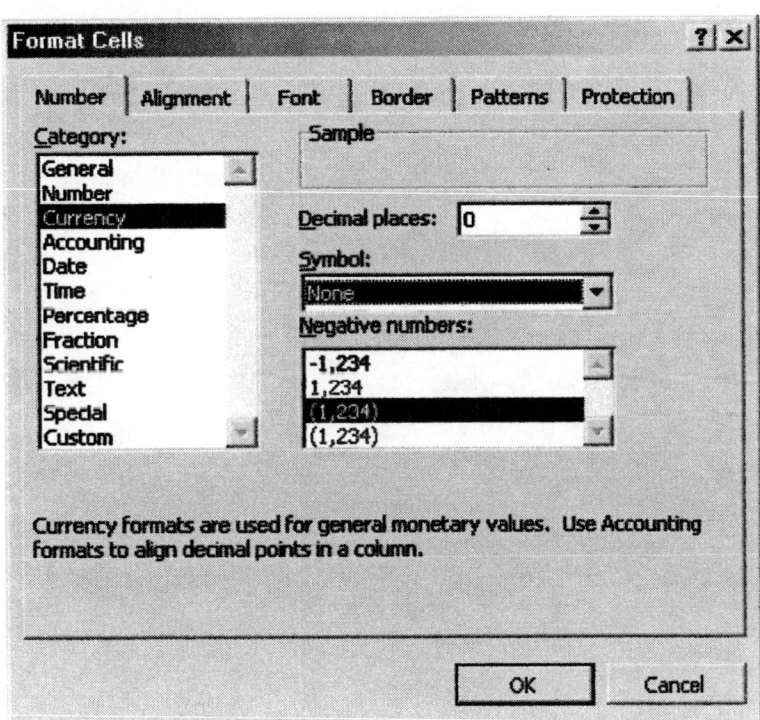

10. Your completed spreadsheet should look like this:

	A	B	C	D	E	F	G	H	I	J
1	Date	Description	Cash +	Other assets =		Liabilities +	Contributed capital +		Retained earnings	
2	2/1/2001	Owner investment	2,000					2,000		
3	2/3/2001	Purchase shirts	(1,200)	1,200	Inventory					
4	2/5/2001	Sale of 100 shirts at $10 each	1,000						1,000	Sales
5		Cost of shirts sold		(400)					(400)	COGS
6	2/25/2001	Paid phone bill	(30)						(30)	Phone expense
7	2/28/2001	Purchase equipment		600	Equipment	600	Accounts Payable			
8										

How to print your spreadsheet

11. Print your file by clicking the **Print** button 🖨. If you want to adjust your printer properties, print by selecting **File, Print** from the menu bar.

How to save your spreadsheet

12. Save your file to disk by clicking the **Save** button 💾. Name your file TomsWear1.

How to close Excel

13. Close Excel by selecting **File, Exit** from the menu bar.

Excel Workshop

CHAPTER 2

Preparing a Statement of Changes in Stockholders' Equity

Before beginning this assignment, read Parts A & B of the Computerized Accounting appendix at the back of this book.

Open Excel

1. Click on the Start button. Point to Programs: select Microsoft Excel. Your desktop may have an Excel icon that allows you to enter the program by double-clicking it.

2. Follow the instructions in Part A of the Computerized Accounting appendix at the back of this book to open a new Excel workbook.

3. The following is a copy of Tom's Wear Statement of Changes in Shareholders' Equity as for the month ending February 28, 2001.

Tom's Wear, Inc.
Statement of Changes in Shareholders' Equity
For the Month Ending February 28, 2001

Beginning contributed capital	$5,000	
Common stock issued during the month	-0-	
Ending contributed capital		$5,000
Beginning retained earnings	$385	
Net income for the month	935	
Dividends	(100)	
Ending retained earnings		1,220
Total shareholders' equity		$6,220

For this problem, assume that in the month of March:
- Tom was issued additional common stock for a $1,000 contribution.
- Total revenue for the month was $2,560
- Total expenses for the month were $1,150
- Tom was paid a dividend of $150

Center text

4. Beginning in cell A1, input appropriate heading lines for a Statement of Changes in Shareholders' Equity. Highlight the cells to be centered and click the **Merge and Center** button ▦ to center your heading lines across columns A – C. Each line must be centered separately. (The second line will appear in full after your column widths are increased.)

5. Input the appropriate dollar amounts in column B and the appropriate totals in column C. Always use formulas when you calculate totals. For example, Ending contributed capital =B5+B6. Instead of typing your formulas, try the click method. Click cell C7 and type " = ". Click cell B5, type "+", click on cell B6 and hit enter.

6. Click **the Increase Indent** button 📝 to indent the words "Total shareholders' equity" within the cell.

7. Format the appropriate cells with $ by clicking the cells and the **Currency Style** button 🔲. Format the other numbers using the **Comma Style** button 🔲. Highlight all the numbers and click the **Decrease Decimal** button 🔲 twice to round the numbers to whole dollars.

8. Underline or double underline the appropriate cells by selecting **Format, Cells, Border**.

9. Your completed spreadsheet should look like this:

	A	B	C
1	Tom's Wear, Inc.		
2	Statement of Changes in Stockholders' Equity		
3	For the month ended March 31, 2001		
4			
5	Beginning contributed capital	$ 5,000	
6	Common stock issued during the month	1,000	
7	Ending contributed capital		$ 6,000
8			
9	Beginning retained earnings	1,220	
10	Net income for the month	1,410	
11	Dividends	(150)	
12	Ending retained earnings		2,480
13	Total shareholders' equity		$ 8,480
14			

10. Print your file by clicking the **Print** button 🖨. If you want to adjust your printer properties, print by selecting **File, Print** from the menu bar.

11. Save your file to disk by clicking the **Save** button 💾. Name your file TomsWear2.

12. Close Excel by selecting **File, Exit** from the menu bar.

CHAPTER 3

Preparing adjustments, an Income Statement, and a Balance Sheet

Before beginning this assignment, read Parts A & B of the Computerized Accounting appendix at the back of this book.

Open Excel

1. Click on the Start button. Point to Programs: select Microsoft Excel. Your desktop may have an Excel icon that allows you to enter the program by double-clicking it.

2. Follow the instructions in Part A of the Computerized Accounting appendix at the back of this book to open a new Excel workbook.

3. Create the following **Bold** **B** column headings beginning in Cell A1 and ending in Cell D1: **Account, Current Balance, Balance Increases, Balance Decreases, Adjusted Balance.** In order to minimize the column width of columns that have multi-word headings, select Format, Cells, Alignment and check the "Wrap Text" box.

4. The following is a is a list of accounts for Tom's Wear, Inc. at March 31, after adjustments:

Cash	$ 3,995
Accounts receivable	2,000
Prepaid insurance	75
Inventory	300
Computer, net of depreciation	3,900
Notes payable	3,000
Interest payable	30
Contributed capital	5,000
Retained earnings, March 1	1,220
Sales	2,000
Cost of goods sold	800
Depreciation expense	100
Insurance expense	50
Interest expense	30

Assume the following additional transactions occurred during the month of March:

A) On March 31, Tom paid $150 in cash for 3 months of advertising in a college newspaper. The ad will appear in the newspaper in the months of April and May

B) Tom hired an employee who started work on March 26th. Tom owes him $80 for March wages. They will be paid April 2nd. (Ignore payroll taxes.)

C) On March 31, a customer ordered some special logo t-shirts and gave Tom a $200 deposit. The t-shirts will be delivered in April.

D) Tom estimates that he will owe $50 in income taxes for March.

5. Beginning in cell A3, enter the account information given above in the **Account** and **Current Balance** columns beginning in cell A3.

6. Enter the adjustment amounts indicated in items A) – D). Add additional accounts as needed.

How to input and copy formulas

7. Complete the process by computing the adjusted balances. Compute the balance for the first account by adding the amount in column B to column C and subtracting column D. For example cell E3 input should be "=B3+C3-D4." Type your formulas or use the click method. Use the fill handle to copy the formulas to the remaining accounts. Select the cell you want to copy and point to the fill handle. When the arrow changes to a thin crosshair, click your left mouse button and drag the handle over the range that you want copied. Release the mouse button to finish.

fill handle   crosshair

8. Your spreadsheet should look like this after all adjustments are completed:

	A	B	C	D	E
1	Account	Current Balance	Balance Increases	Balance Decreases	Adjusted Balance
2					
3	Cash	$ 3,995	$ 200	$ 150	$ 4,045
4	Accounts receivable	$ 2,000			2,000
5	Prepaid insurance	75			75
6	Inventory	300			300
7	Computer, net of depreciation	3,900			3,900
8	Notes payable	3,000			3,000
9	Interest payable	30			30
10	Contributed capital	5,000			5,000
11	Retained earnings, March 1	1,220			1,220
12	Sales	2,000			2,000
13	Cost of goods sold	800			800
14	Depreciation expense	100			100
15	Insurance expense	50			50
16	Interest expense	30			30
17	Prepaid advertising	0	150		150
18	Wages expense	0	80		80
19	Wages payable	0	80		80
20	Unearned revenue	0	200		200
21	Taxes expense	0	50		50
22	Taxes payable	0	50		50

9. Beginning in cell G1, input appropriate heading lines for an Income Statement. Highlight the cells to be centered and click the **Merge and Center** button ▦ to center your heading lines across columns G - I. Each line must be centered separately.

10. Beginning in cell G5, prepare an income statement for the month ended March 31. Adjust the column widths as needed. Input the account names and dollar amounts input by referencing cells. For example, "=B12" for sales or "= E12" for the sales balance. Remember to use formulas when you add columns of numbers.

11. Use the **Increase Indent** ⇥ button to indent the totals. Format the appropriate cells with $ by clicking the cells and the **Currency Style** button **$**. Format the other numbers using the **Comma Style** button **,**. Highlight all the numbers and click the **Decrease Decimal** button ⁰⁰ twice to round the numbers to whole dollars. Underline or double underline the appropriate cells by selecting **Format, Cells, Border**.

12. Your completed income statement should look like this:

	G	H	I
1	Tom's Wear, Inc.		
2	Income Statement		
3	For the Month Ended March 31, 2001		
4			
5	Sales revenue		$ 2,000
6			
7	Expenses:		
8	Cost of goods sold	$ 800	
9	Depreciation expense	100	
10	Insurance expense	50	
11	Interest expense	30	
12	Wages expense	80	
13	Taxes expense	50	
14	Total Expense		$ 1,110
15			
16	Net Income		$ 890

13. Beginning in cell G21, input appropriate heading lines for a balance sheet for March 31, 2001. Follow the formatting instructions in step 9.

14. Click the **Italic** button *I* and type "Assets" in cell G25. Repeat and type "Liabilities and Equity" in cell J25.

Use cell referencing to avoid repetition

15. Beginning in cells G26 and J26, prepare a balance sheet for the month ended March 31. Adjust the column widths as needed. Input the account names and dollar amounts input by referencing cells. For example, "=A3" for cash or "= E3" for the cash balance. Remember to use formulas when you add columns of numbers. Format your balance sheet as discussed in step 10, above.

16. Your completed balance sheet should look like this:

	G	H	I	J	K	L
20						
21				Tom's Wear, Inc.		
22				Balance Sheet		
23				March 31, 2001		
24						
25	Assets:			Liabilities and Equity:		
26	Cash	$ 4,045		Liabilities:		
27	Accounts receivable	2,000		Wages payable	$ 80	
28	Prepaid insurance	75		Unearned revenue	200	
29	Prepaid advertising	150		Taxes payable	50	
30	Inventory	300		Interest payable	30	
31	Computer, net of depreciation	3,900		Notes payable	3,000	
32				Total liabilities		$ 3,360
33	Total assets	$ 10,470				
34				Stockholders' equity		
35				Contributed capital	$ 5,000	
36				Retained earnings	2,110	
37				Total equity		$ 7,110
38						
39				Total liabilities and equity		$ 10,470

Print your spreadsheet

17. Print your file by clicking the **Print** button 🖨. If you want to adjust your printer properties, print by selecting **File, Print** from the menu bar.

Save your spreadsheet

18. Save your file to disk by clicking the **Save** button 💾. Name your file TomsWear3.

Close Excel

19. Close Excel by selecting **File, Exit** from the menu bar.

CHAPTER 4

Preparing Closing Entries and a Postclosing Trial Balance

Before beginning this assignment, read Parts A & B of the Computerized Accounting appendix at the back of this book. Note: This is the only chapter that contains debits and credits and is related to the closing process. If the topic is not being covered, this chapter may be skipped.

Open Excel

1. Click on the Start button. Point to Programs: select Microsoft Excel. Your desktop may have an Excel icon that allows you to enter the program by double-clicking it.

2. Follow the instructions in Part A of the Computerized Accounting appendix at the back of this book to open a new Excel workbook.

3. Input the following **Bold** **B** column headings beginning in cell A1 and ending in cell E1: **Ref., Date, Journal Entry, DR, CR.**

4. The following is Tom's Wear, Inc. Adjusted Trial Balance at March 31, 2001.

Tom's Wear, Inc. Adjusted Trial Balance March 31, 2001		
	Debit	**Credit**
Cash	$3,995	
Accounts receivable	2,000	
Inventory	300	
Prepaid insurance	75	
Computer	4,000	
Accumulated depreciation		100
Interest payable		30
Notes payable		3,000
Common stock		5,000
Retained earnings		1,220
Sales		2,000
Cost of goods sold	800	
Insurance expense	50	
Depreciation expense	100	
Interest expense	30	
Totals	$11,350	$11,350

For purposes of this problem, assume that Tom's Wear, Inc. is closing the books for the month of March. Enter the necessary closing entries. Adjust your column widths as needed.

5. Prepare a post closing trial balance for Tom's Wear, Inc. Use appropriate headings and formatting. To sum the total debits and credits select the appropriate cell and click the **Auto Sum** Σ button.

6. Your completed spreadsheet should look like this:

	A	B	C	D	E
1	**Ref.**	**Date**	**Journal Entry**	**DR**	**CR**
2	c-1	3/31	Sales	2,000	
3			Retained earnings		2,000
4			To close the Sales account.		
5					
6	c-2	3/31	Retained earnings	980	
7			Cost of goods sold		800
8			Insurance expense		50
9			Depreciation expense		100
10			Interest expense		30
11			To close the expense accounts.		
12					
13			Post Closing Trial Balance		
14			**Account**	**DR**	**CR**
15			Cash	3,995	
16			Accounts receivable	2,000	
17			Inventory	300	
18			Prepaid insurance	75	
19			Computer	4,000	
20			Accumulated depreciation		100
21			Interest payable		30
22			Notes payable		3,000
23			Common stock		5,000
24			Retained earnings		2,240
25				10,370	10,370

7. Print your file by clicking the **Print** button 🖨. If you want to adjust your printer properties, print by selecting **File, Print** from the menu bar.

8. Save your file to disk by clicking the **Save** button 💾. Name your file TomsWear4.

9. Close Excel by selecting **File, Exit** from the menu bar.

CHAPTER 5

Preparing a Depreciation Schedule

Before beginning this assignment, read Parts A & B of the Computerized Accounting appendix at the back of this book.

Open Excel

1. Click on the Start button. Point to Programs: select Microsoft Excel. Your desktop may have an Excel icon that allows you to enter the program by double-clicking it.

2. Follow the instructions in Part A of the Computerized Accounting appendix at the back of this book to open a new Excel workbook.

How to use the Align Right button to format headings

3. Input the following **Bold** **B** column headings beginning in cell A1 and ending in cell E1: **Year, Beginning Book Value, Current Depreciation Expense, Accumulated Depreciation, Ending Book Value.** Use Format, Cells, Alignment and "Wrap Text" in order to minimize the column width of columns that have multi-word headings. Click the **Align Right** button to align all the column headings.

4. Tom's Wear, Inc. purchased a new van for $30,000. The purpose of this exercise is to prepare a depreciation schedule for three methods of depreciation: Straight-Line, Units of Production and Double Declining Balance. Assume a 5-year or 50,000 mile estimated useful life, a full year's depreciation will be taken in the year of purchase and that the van will have no salvage value. For Units of Production assume that the following mileage breakdown: Year 1: 5,000 miles; Year 2: 15,000 miles; Year 3: 12,000 miles; Year 4: 10,000 miles and Year 5: 8,000 miles. For Double Declining Balance, assume that the full undepreciated book value at the end of year 4 will be taken as depreciation expense in year 5.

Italicize headings

5. Prepare depreciation schedules for the three methods of depreciation discussed above. Put the headings in column B, row 3 (Straight-Line), row 11 (Units of Production) and row 19 (Double Declining Balance). Click the **Italics** button *I* before typing to italicize headings.

How to copy cells using the Copy and Paste buttons

6. Use formulas to calculate Current Depreciation Expense, Accumulated Depreciation and Ending Book Value. Many of the formulas needed may be input once and copied. For example, Beginning Book Value – Current Depreciation Expense = Ending Book Value. Input the formula one time for each schedule and then copy it to the other years either by using the fill handle or by clicking the Copy and Paste buttons.

7. Your completed spreadsheet should look like this:

	A	B	C	D	E
1	Year	Beginning Book Value	Current Depreciation Expense	Accumulated Depreciation	Ending Book Value
2					
3		*Straight-Line*			
4	1	$30,000	$6,000	$6,000	$24,000
5	2	$24,000	$6,000	$12,000	$18,000
6	3	$18,000	$6,000	$18,000	$12,000
7	4	$12,000	$6,000	$24,000	$6,000
8	5	$6,000	$6,000	$30,000	$0
9					
10					
11		*Units of Production*			
12	1	$30,000	$3,000	$3,000	$27,000
13	2	$27,000	$9,000	$12,000	$18,000
14	3	$18,000	$7,200	$19,200	$10,800
15	4	$10,800	$6,000	$25,200	$4,800
16	5	$4,800	$4,800	$30,000	$0
17					
18					
19		*Double Declining Balance*			
20	1	$30,000	$12,000	$12,000	$18,000
21	2	$18,000	$7,200	$19,200	$10,800
22	3	$10,800	$4,320	$23,520	$6,480
23	4	$6,480	$2,592	$26,112	$3,888
24	5	$3,888	$3,888	$30,000	$0

Print your spreadsheet

8. Print your file by clicking the **Print** button. If you want to adjust your printer properties, print by selecting **File, Print** from the menu bar.

Save your spreadsheet

9. Save your file to disk by clicking the **Save** button. Name your file TomsWear5.

Close Excel

10. Close Excel by selecting **File, Exit** from the menu bar.

CHAPTER 6

Preparing Inventory Schedules and Computing Net Income Under Various Inventory Methods

Before beginning this assignment, read Parts A & B of the Computerized Accounting appendix at the back of this book.

Open Excel

1. Click on the Start button. Point to Programs: select Microsoft Excel. Your desktop may have an Excel icon that allows you to enter the program by double-clicking it.

2. Follow the instructions in Part A of the Computerized Accounting appendix at the back of this book to open a new Excel workbook.

3. Assume that in the month of May, Tom's Wear engaged in the following transactions:

   5/01/2001 Beginning Inventory: 500 shirts @ $4.00 each
   5/03/2001 Tom purchased 300 shirts for $4.10 each.
   5/05/2001 Tom sold 600 shirts for $10.50 each.
   5/15/2001 Tom purchased 400 shirts for $4.20 each.
   5/18/2001 Tom sold 400 shirts for $10.50 each
   5/28/2001 Tom purchased 200 shirts for $4.25 each
   5/30/2001 Tom sold 100 shirts for $10.50 each

   Tom uses a periodic inventory system.

How to use Auto Sum to add numbers

4. Beginning in cell A1, input the following chart based on the information presented above. Input or calculate the values for the highlighted cells. (You do not need to highlight the cells.) To sum the total goods available for sale, click on the appropriate cell C6 or E6 and click the Auto Sum **Σ** button. Select Format, Cells, Number and Date to format column A.

	A	B	C	D	E
1	Date	Activity	Units	Unit Cost	Total Cost
2					
3	1-May-01	Beginning balance			
4	3-May-01	Purchase			
5	15-May-01	Purchase			
6	28-May-01	Purchase			
7		Total goods available for sale			
8		Shirts sold			
9		Shirts in ending inventory			

5. Calculate cost of goods sold and ending inventory under the FIFO, LIFO and weighted average methods. Use formulas and the information entered in cells A1 through E8 to calculate the amounts. ,

	A	B	C	D
12		FIFO	LIFO	Weighted Average
13	Cost of goods sold			
14	Ending inventory			
15				

6. Calculate the net income under each of the three methods, by inputting the following schedule. Assume that operating expenses were 3,500 and income taxes are computed at 30%. Remember to use formulas where applicable and to copy cost of goods sold from row 13 using the Copy 📋 and Paste 📋 buttons.

	A	B	C	D
17	Income Statements	FIFO	LIFO	Weighted Average
18				
19	Sales			
20	Cost of goods sold			
21	Gross profit			
22	Operating expenses			
23	Income before taxes			
24	Income taxes			
25	Income after tax			

7. Your completed spreadsheet should look like this:

	A	B	C	D	E
1	Date	Activity	Units	Unit Cost	Total Cost
2					
3	1-May-01	Beginning balance	500	$4.00	$ 2,000
4	3-May-01	Purchase	300	$4.10	$ 1,230
5	15-May-01	Purchase	400	$4.20	$ 1,680
6	28-May-01	Purchase	200	$4.25	$ 850
7		Total goods available for sale	1,400		$ 5,760
8		Shirts sold	1,100		
9		Shirts in ending inventory	300		
10					
11					
12		FIFO	LIFO	Weighted Average	
13	Cost of goods sold	$4,490	$4,560	$4,526	
14	Ending inventory	1,270	1,200	1,234	

- 16 -

	A	B	C	D
17	**Income Statements**	**FIFO**	**LIFO**	**Weighted Average**
18				
19	Sales	$11,550	$11,550	$11,550
20	Cost of goods sold	4,490	4,560	4,526
21	Gross profit	$7,060	$6,990	$7,024
22	Operating expenses	3,500	3,500	3,500
23	Income before taxes	$3,560	$3,490	$3,524
24	Income taxes	1,068	1,047	1,057
25	Income after tax	$2,492	$2,443	$2,467

Print your spreadsheet

8. Print your file by clicking the **Print** button 🖨. If you want to adjust your printer properties, print by selecting **File, Print** from the menu bar.

Save your spreadsheet

9. Save your file to disk by clicking the **Save** button 💾. Name your file TomsWear6.

Close Excel

10. Close Excel by selecting **File, Exit** from the menu bar.

CHAPTER 7

Preparing an Accounts Receivable Aging Schedule

Before beginning this assignment, read Parts A & B of the Computerized Accounting appendix at the back of this book.

Open Excel

1. Click on the Start button. Point to Programs: select Microsoft Excel. Your desktop may have an Excel icon that allows you to enter the program by double-clicking it.

2. Follow the instructions in Part A of the Computerized Accounting appendix at the back of this book to open a new Excel workbook.

3. Beginning in cell B1, input the following chart. Resize columns and wrap text as needed. You can improve the appearance of a worksheet by changing the font type and sizes and by adding color. Formatting tips to improve the appearance of your chart are given after the chart.

	A	B	C	D	E	F
1		Tom's Wear, Inc.				
2		Accounts Receivable Aging Schedule				
3		July 31, 2001				
4						
5		Age Group	Amount		Estimated Percent Uncollectible	Estimated Allowance
6		0 - 30 days			2%	
7		31 - 60 days			3%	
8		61 - 90 days			10%	
9		91 - 120 days			15%	
10		Over 120 days			40%	
11						
12						
13						

How to change font type and size

4. Change the font type and size by using the pull-down menus on the toolbar. To change a large area, highlight the cells you want to change before selecting the font and size. Select Tahoma or any other font you prefer.

How to add color to your spreadsheet

5. To change the color of selected areas of a spreadsheet, highlight the area(s) to be changed and select **Format, Cells, Patterns** from the menu and choose the color of your choice. Colors can be layered. In other words, highlight A1 to G15 and choose white. Next, highlight B5 to F12 and choose light yellow (or any other color you prefer).

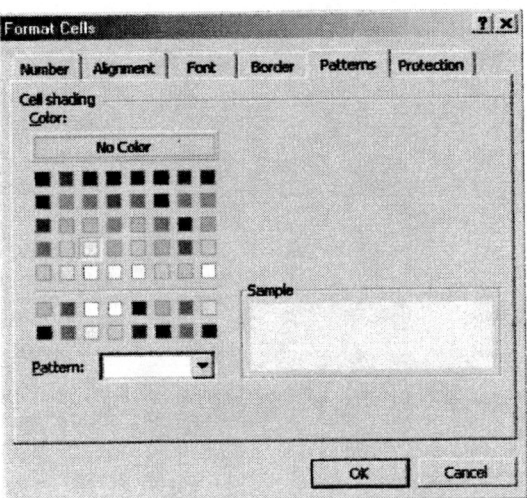

6. At the end of June, Tom's Wear, Inc.'s accounts receivable balance was as follows:

Accounts receivable	$44,100
Less: allowance	(1,320)
Net accounts receivable	$42,780

Tom's July sales totaled $99,000 (all on account), $37,000 of Accounts receivable were collected and $1,000 was written off as uncollectible. Based on this information, calculate the balance of Accounts receivable and the Allowance account at the end of July before the adjustment for bad debts.

7. Assume for this problem that Tom has done an aging of his July 31 accounts receivable balance and determined the following:

Accounts due in	% of total accounts receivable
0 – 30 days	55%
31 – 60 days	30%
61 – 90 days	10%
90 – 120 days	4%
Over 120 days	1%
	100%

Based upon your calculations from step 3, determine the dollar amount for each category in the aging schedule and complete the aging schedule. Remember to use formulas where appropriate.

8. Beginning in cell B17, input and complete the following information at July 31, 2001:

Accounts receivable	$_____
Less: allowance	(_____)
Net accounts receivable	$_____

All of these numbers should be calculated using formulas. Use the information from your aging schedule to create a formula for accounts receivable.

9. Your completed spreadsheet should look like this:

	A	B	C	D	E	F
1		Tom's Wear, Inc.				
2		Accounts Receivable Aging Schedule				
3		July 31, 2001				
4						
5		Age Group		Amount	Estimated Percent Uncollectible	Estimated Allowance
6		0 - 30 days		$57,805.00	2%	$1,156.10
7		31 - 60 days		$31,530.00	3%	$945.90
8		61 - 90 days		$10,510.00	10%	$1,051.00
9		91 - 120 days		$4,204.00	15%	$630.60
10		Over 120 days		$1,051.00	40%	$420.40
11						$4,204.00
12						
13						
14						
15						
16						
17		Accounts Receivable		$105,100		
18		Less: Allowance for Doubtful Accounts		$4,204		
19		Net Accounts Receivable		$100,896		

Print your spreadsheet

10. Print your file by clicking the **Print** button 🖨. If you want to adjust your printer properties, print by selecting **File, Print** from the menu bar.

Save your spreadsheet

11. Save your file to disk by clicking the **Save** button 💾. Name your file TomsWear7.

Close Excel

12. Close Excel by selecting **File, Exit** from the menu bar.

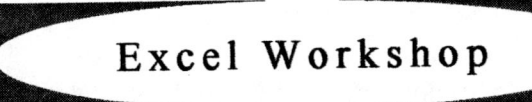

Excel Workshop

CHAPTER 6

Preparing Inventory Schedules and Computing Net Income Under Various Inventory Methods

Before beginning this assignment, read Parts A & B of the Computerized Accounting appendix at the back of this book.

Open Excel

1. Click on the Start button. Point to Programs: select Microsoft Excel. Your desktop may have an Excel icon that allows you to enter the program by double-clicking it.

2. Follow the instructions in Part A of the Computerized Accounting appendix at the back of this book to open a new Excel workbook.

3. Assume that in the month of May, Tom's Wear engaged in the following transactions:

   5/01/2001 Beginning Inventory: 500 shirts @ $4.00 each
   5/03/2001 Tom purchased 300 shirts for $4.10 each.
   5/05/2001 Tom sold 600 shirts for $10.50 each.
   5/15/2001 Tom purchased 400 shirts for $4.20 each.
   5/18/2001 Tom sold 400 shirts for $10.50 each
   5/28/2001 Tom purchased 200 shirts for $4.25 each
   5/30/2001 Tom sold 100 shirts for $10.50 each

   Tom uses a periodic inventory system.

How to use Auto Sum to add numbers

4. Beginning in cell A1, input the following chart based on the information presented above. Input or calculate the values for the highlighted cells. (You do not need to highlight the cells.) To sum the total goods available for sale, click on the appropriate cell C6 or E6 and click the **Auto Sum** Σ button. Select Format, Cells, Number and Date to format column A.

	A	B	C	D	E
1	Date	Activity	Units	Unit Cost	Total Cost
2					
3	1-May-01	Beginning balance			
4	3-May-01	Purchase			
5	15-May-01	Purchase			
6	28-May-01	Purchase			
7		Total goods available for sale			
8		Shirts sold			
9		Shirts in ending inventory			

5. Calculate cost of goods sold and ending inventory under the FIFO, LIFO and weighted average methods. Use formulas and the information entered in cells A1 through E8 to calculate the amounts.

	A	B	C	D
12		FIFO	LIFO	Weighted Average
13	Cost of goods sold			
14	Ending inventory			
15				

6. Calculate the net income under each of the three methods, by inputting the following schedule. Assume that operating expenses were 3,500 and income taxes are computed at 30%. Remember to use formulas where applicable and to copy cost of goods sold from row 13 using the **Copy** 📋 and **Paste** 📋 buttons.

	A	B	C	D
17	Income Statements	FIFO	LIFO	Weighted Average
18				
19	Sales			
20	Cost of goods sold			
21	Gross profit			
22	Operating expenses			
23	Income before taxes			
24	Income taxes			
25	Income after tax			

7. Your completed spreadsheet should look like this:

	A	B	C	D	E
1	Date	Activity	Units	Unit Cost	Total Cost
2					
3	1-May-01	Beginning balance	500	$4.00	$ 2,000
4	3-May-01	Purchase	300	$4.10	$ 1,230
5	15-May-01	Purchase	400	$4.20	$ 1,680
6	28-May-01	Purchase	200	$4.25	$ 850
7		Total goods available for sale	1,400		$ 5,760
8		Shirts sold	1,100		
9		Shirts in ending inventory	300		
10					
11					
12		FIFO	LIFO	Weighted Average	
13	Cost of goods sold	$4,490	$4,560	$4,526	
14	Ending inventory	1,270	1,200	1,234	

- 16 -

9. To improve the appearance of your printout, select **File, Page Setup, Margins** and check the Center on page horizontally box. This will not change what you see on your screen, but will center the output when you print your file.

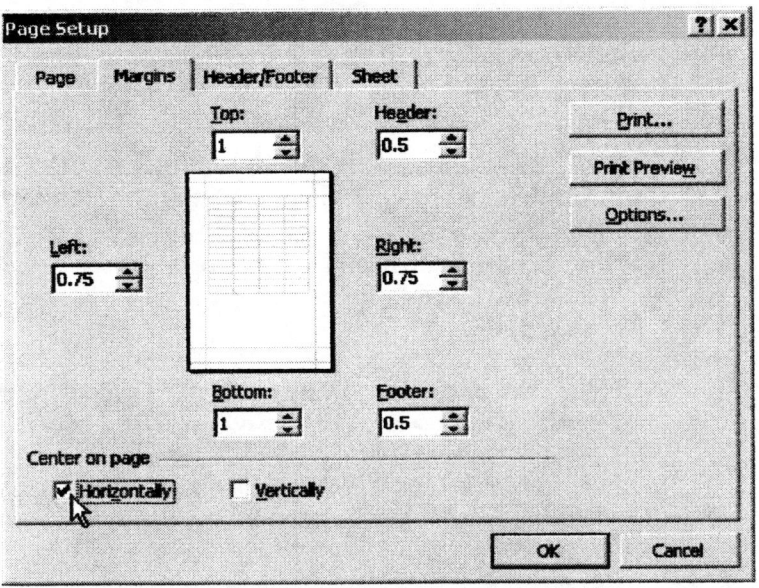

Print your spreadsheet

10. Print your file by clicking the **Print button** ⎙ . If you want to adjust your printer properties, print by selecting **File, Print** from the menu bar. Your (partial) printout should appear as follows:

Student Name	Accounting 1	2/9/2002

Tom's Wear, Inc.
Stockholders' Equity
at September 30, 2001

Preferred stock (10,000 shares authorized, 1,000 shares issued and outstanding)	$	100,000
Common stock (50,000,000 shares authorized, 787,500 shares issued and outstanding)		7,875
Additional paid-in-capital		1,331,000
Retained earnings		105,586
Total shareholders' equity	$	1,544,461

Save your spreadsheet

11. Save your file to disk by clicking the **Save button** 💾 . Name your file TomsWear9.

Close Excel

12. Close Excel by selecting **File, Exit** from the menu bar.

CHAPTER 10

Preparing a Statement of Cash Flow and Changing Print Formats

Before beginning this assignment, read Parts A & B of the Computerized Accounting appendix at the back of this book.

Open Excel

1. Click on the Start button. Point to Programs: select Microsoft Excel. Your desktop may have an Excel icon that allows you to enter the program by double-clicking it.

2. Follow the instructions in Part A of the Computerized Accounting appendix at the back of this book to open a new Excel workbook.

3. In this exercise, you will prepare a Statement of Cash Flow and work with some additional Excel formatting option.

4. Beginning in cell A1, input the following chart. Resize columns and wrap text as required. You may also choose the font type and size as desired. Use appropriate formulas to calculate the change in the balances. Tom did not sell any long-term assets or pay any dividends during the month.

	A	B	C	D
1		July 31, 2001	August 31, 2001	Change
2	Assets			
3	Cash	$ 17,151	$ 980,476	$ 963,325
4	Accounts receivable	105,100	207,610	102,510
5	Allowance for doubtful accounts	(3,290)	(6,335)	(3,045)
6	Inventory	8,910	24,584	15,674
7	Prepaids	800	700	(100)
8	Land	7,500	7,500	-
9	Equipment	4,000	104,000	100,000
10	Accumulated depr., equipment	(500)	(600)	(100)
11	Van	30,000	130,000	100,000
12	Accumulated depr., van	(4,205)	(7,105)	(2,900)
13	Building	67,500	67,500	-
14	Accumulated depr., building	(130)	(260)	(130)
15	Total Assets	$ 232,836	$ 1,508,070	$ 1,275,234
16				

(Chart is continued at the top of the next page)

Print your spreadsheet

17. Print your file by clicking the **Print** button ⊟. If you want to adjust your printer properties, print by selecting **File, Print** from the menu bar.

Save your spreadsheet

18. Save your file to disk by clicking the **Save** button ⊟. Name your file TomsWear8.

Close Excel

19. Close Excel by selecting **File, Exit** from the menu bar.

Excel Workshop

CHAPTER 9

Preparing a Statement of Changes in Stockholders' Equity and Changing Prints Formats

Before beginning this assignment, read Parts A & B of the Computerized Accounting appendix at the back of this book.

Open Excel

1. Click on the Start button. Point to Programs: select Microsoft Excel. Your desktop may have an Excel icon that allows you to enter the program by double-clicking it.

2. Follow the instructions in Part A of the Computerized Accounting appendix at the back of this book to open a new Excel workbook.

3. In this exercise, you will prepare a Statement of Changes in Stockholders' Equity for Tom's Wear, Inc. and work with some Excel formatting option.

4. The following is a copy of Tom's Wear, Inc.'s stockholders' equity section of the balance sheet at August 31, 2001:

Common stock ($.01 par value, 50,000,000 shares authorized, 750,000 shares issued and outstanding)	$ 7,500
Additional paid-in-capital	1,247,000
Retained earnings	136,616
Total stockholders' equity	$1,391,116

For purposes of this problem only, assume that in the month of September:

- Tom was authorized to sell 10,000 shares of $100 par, 6% preferred stock.
- Tom sold 1,000 shares of the preferred stock at its par value.
- A cash dividend of $1.00 per share was paid to the preferred stockholders.
- Tom declared and issued a 5% stock dividend on the common stock when the market value of the stock was $2.25.
- Net income for the month was $54,345.

5. Beginning in cell A1, input the stockholders' equity section of Tom's Wear, Inc.'s balance sheet. Use appropriate formatting. Calculate the appropriate balances of the stockholders' equity accounts as of September 30, 2001, based upon the information presented above. Show all work and use formulas as appropriate. Place your calculations under the stockholders' equity section. Use appropriate labels, formatting, and formulas. Your worksheet should look like what is shown on the top of the next page:

	A	B
1	Tom's Wear, Inc.	
2	Stockholders' Equity	
3	at September 30, 2001	
4		
5	Preferred stock (shares authorized, shares issued and outstanding)	
6	Common stock (shares authorized, shares issued and outstanding)	
7	Additional paid-in-capital	
8	Retained earnings	
9	Total shareholders' equity	$ -
10		
11	*Calculations:*	
12	Beginning common stock	
13	Stock dividend %	
14		
15	Market value	
16	Value of stock dividend	
17		
18	Par value of common stock	
19	New shares issued	
20	Increase in common stock account	
21		
22	Increase in additional paid in capital account ($ - $)	
23		
24	Total shares of common stock oustanding at September 30, 2001 (+)	
25		
26	Retained earnings calculation:	
27	Beginning balance	
28	Net income	
29	Cash dividends	
30	Stock dividend	
31	Ending retained earnings	

6. Input the numbers you calculated into the equity section using formulas as appropriate.

**How to add a
header to your
worksheet**

7. Add a header to your worksheet by selecting **File, Page Setup** from the menu bar. Select **Header/Footer** and **Custom Header.** Input your name and class as shown below. Click the date button to put the date in the right section.

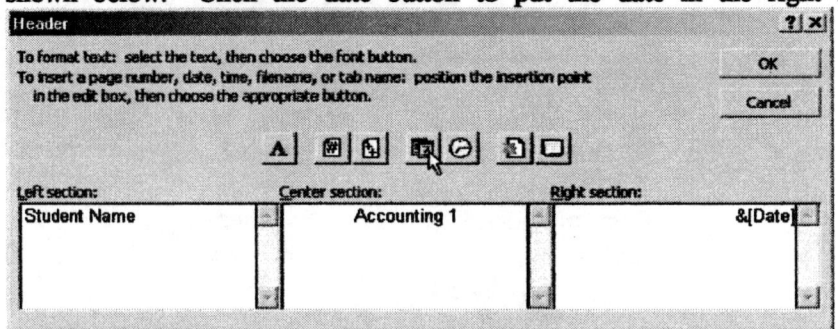

8. Your completed spreadsheet should look like this:

	A	B	C
1	Tom's Wear, Inc.		
2	Stockholders' Equity		
3	at September 30, 2001		
4			
5	Preferred stock (10,000 shares authorized, 1,000 shares issued and outstanding)	$ 100,000	
6	Common stock (50,000,000 shares authorized, 787,500 shares issued and outstanding)	7,875	
7	Additional paid-in-capital	1,331,000	
8	Retained earnings	105,586	
9	Total shareholders' equity	$ 1,544,461	
10			
11	*Calculations:*		
12	Beginning common stock	750,000	shares
13	Stock dividend %	5%	
14		37,500	new shares
15	Market value	$ 2.25	
16	Value of stock dividend	$ 84,375	
17			
18	Par value of common stock	0.01	
19	New shares issued	37,500	
20	Increase in common stock account	$ 375	
21			
22	Increase in additional paid in capital account ($84,375 - 375)	$ 84,000	
23			
24	Total shares of common stock oustanding at September 30, 2001 (750,000 + 37,500)	787,500	
25			
26	Retained earnings calculation:		
27	Beginning balance	$ 136,616	
28	Net income	54,345	
29	Cash dividends	(1,000)	
30	Stock dividend	(84,375)	
31	Ending retained earnings	$ 105,586	

9. To improve the appearance of your printout, select **File, Page Setup, Margins** and check the Center on page horizontally box. This will not change what you see on your screen, but will center the output when you print your file.

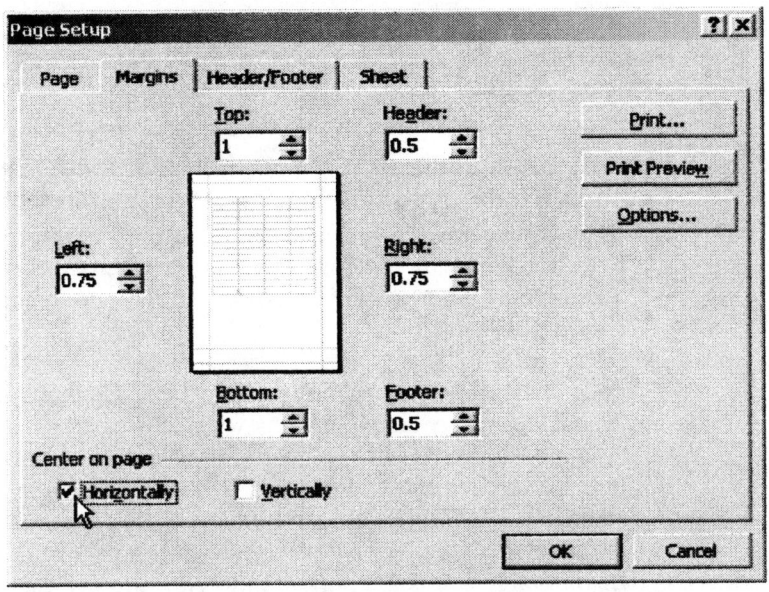

Print your spreadsheet

10. Print your file by clicking the **Print button** ⎙. If you want to adjust your printer properties, print by selecting **File, Print** from the menu bar. Your (partial) printout should appear as follows:

Student Name   Accounting 1   2/9/2002

Tom's Wear, Inc.
Stockholders' Equity
at September 30, 2001

Preferred stock (10,000 shares authorized, 1,000 shares issued and outstanding)	$	100,000
Common stock (60,000,000 shares authorized, 787,500 shares issued and outstanding)		7,875
Additional paid-in-capital		1,331,000
Retained earnings		105,586
Total shareholders' equity	$	1,544,461

Save your spreadsheet

11. Save your file to disk by clicking the **Save button** 💾. Name your file TomsWear9.

Close Excel

12. Close Excel by selecting **File, Exit** from the menu bar.

CHAPTER 10

Preparing a Statement of Cash Flow and Changing Print Formats

Before beginning this assignment, read Parts A & B of the Computerized Accounting appendix at the back of this book.

Open Excel

1. Click on the Start button. Point to Programs: select Microsoft Excel. Your desktop may have an Excel icon that allows you to enter the program by double-clicking it.

2. Follow the instructions in Part A of the Computerized Accounting appendix at the back of this book to open a new Excel workbook.

3. In this exercise, you will prepare a Statement of Cash Flow and work with some additional Excel formatting option.

4. Beginning in cell A1, input the following chart. Resize columns and wrap text as required. You may also choose the font type and size as desired. Use appropriate formulas to calculate the change in the balances. Tom did not sell any long-term assets or pay any dividends during the month.

	A	B	C	D
1		July 31, 2001	August 31, 2001	Change
2	Assets			
3	Cash	$ 17,151	$ 980,476	$ 963,325
4	Accounts receivable	105,100	207,610	102,510
5	Allowance for doubtful accounts	(3,290)	(6,335)	(3,045)
6	Inventory	8,910	24,584	15,674
7	Prepaids	800	700	(100)
8	Land	7,500	7,500	-
9	Equipment	4,000	104,000	100,000
10	Accumulated depr., equipment	(500)	(600)	(100)
11	Van	30,000	130,000	100,000
12	Accumulated depr., van	(4,205)	(7,105)	(2,900)
13	Building	67,500	67,500	-
14	Accumulated depr., building	(130)	(260)	(130)
15	Total Assets	$ 232,836	$ 1,508,070	$ 1,275,234
16				

(Chart is continued at the top of the next page)

	A	B	C	D
17	**Liabilites & Equity**			
18	Accounts payable	$ 36,000	$ 6,000	$ (30,000)
19	Interest payable	1,500	2,250	750
20	Warranty liability	2,239	3,204	965
21	Notes payable	105,000	105,000	-
22	Common stock	5,000	7,500	2,500
23	Additional paid-in capital	0	1,247,500	1,247,500
24	Retained earnings	83,097	136,616	53,519
25	Total Liabilities & Shareholders' Equity	$ 232,836	$ 1,508,070	$ 1,275,234
26				
27	**Income Statement Information:**			
28	Net income		$ 53,519	
29	Depreciation expense		3,130	

5. Beginning in cell F1, prepare a statement of cash flows for Tom's Wear, Inc. for the month ended August 31. Use appropriate headings, formats, and formulas. To change a negative number to a positive (or visa versa), multiple your formula or input cell by "-1." Use parentheses as needed. For example, to calculate depreciation expense for the month the formula is " =(D10+D12+D14)*-1.

6. Your completed cash flow statement should look like this:

	F	G	H	I
1		Tom's Wear, Inc.		
2		Statement of Cash Flows		
3		For the month ended August 31, 2001		
4				
5	**Cash from operating activities**			
6	Net income			$ 53,519
7	Add:	Depreciation expense	3,130	
8		Decrease in prepaids	100	
9		Increase in interest payable	750	
10		Increase in warranty liability	965	
11	Deduct:	Net increase in accounts receivable	(99,465)	
12		Increase in inventory	(15,674)	
13		Decrease in accounts payable	(30,000)	(140,194)
14	Total cash from operating activities			$ (86,675)
15				
16	**Cash from investing activities**			
17	Purchase of fixed assets			(200,000)
18				
19	**Cash from financing activities**			
20	Proceeds from common stock issue			1,250,000
21				
22	**Net increase in cash**			$ 963,325
23	**Beginning cash balance**			17,151
24	**Ending cash balance**			$ 980,476

How to change page layout

7. To change the orientation when you print your spreadsheet, select **File, Page Setup, Page** and check the **Landscape** box. To ensure that the spreadsheet prints on a single 8 1/2 x 11 sheet of paper, check **Fit to 1 page(s) wide by 1 tall.** This will not change what you see on your screen, but it will change how your printout appears.

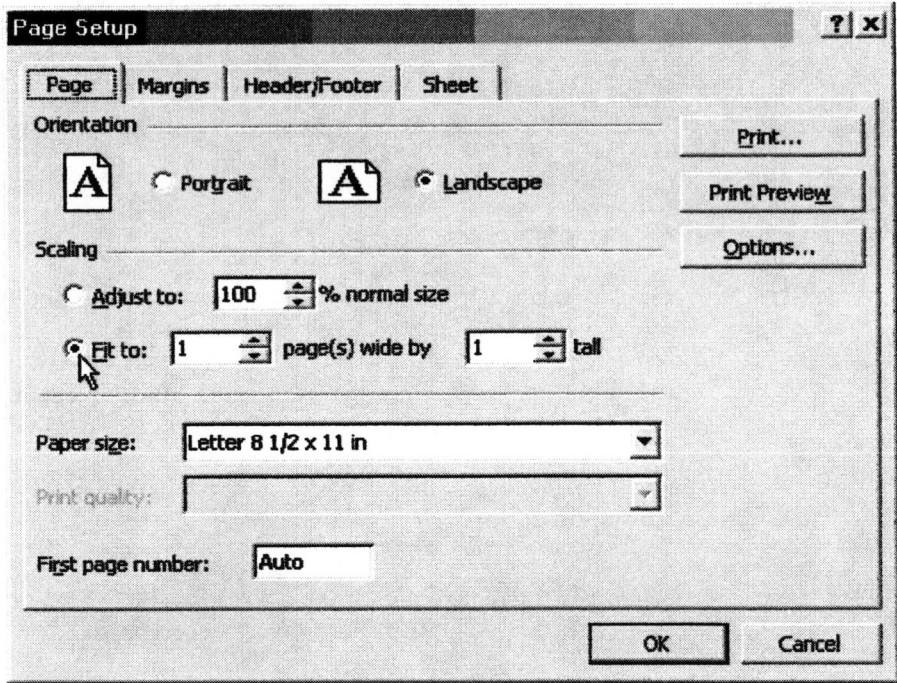

Print your spreadsheet

8. Print your file by clicking **Print** on the **Page Setup** screen. If you want to check how your output will look before printing choose **Print Preview** first.

Save your spreadsheet

9. Save your file to disk by clicking the **Save** button ⊞. Name your file TomsWear10.

Close Excel

10. Close Excel by selecting **File, Exit** from the menu bar.

CHAPTER 11

Preparing a Ratio Analysis and Changing Print Formats

Before beginning this assignment, read Parts A & B of the Computerized Accounting appendix at the back of this book.

Open Excel

1. Click on the Start button. Point to Programs: select Microsoft Excel. Your desktop may have an Excel icon that allows you to enter the program by double-clicking it.

2. Follow the instructions in Part A of the Computerized Accounting appendix at the back of this book to open a new Excel workbook.

3. In this exercise, you will do ratio analysis for Tom's Wear, Inc. and work with some additional Excel formatting option.

4. Beginning in cell A1, input the following chart detailing Tom's Wear, Inc.'s financial statement information at the end of the second and third quarters. Use formulas as appropriate to calculate totals. You may also choose the font type and size as desired.

	A	B	C	D
1				
2	Income statements for the	2nd quarter		3rd quarter
3	Sales revenue	$ 70,700		$ 522,171
4	Cost of goods sold	(25,535)		(177,826)
5	Gross margin	45,165		344,345
6	Interest expense	(810)		(2,250)
7	Other expenses	(11,933)		(185,603)
8	Net income	$ 32,422		$ 156,492
9				
10	Balance sheets at	June 30, 2001		September 30, 2001
11	Assets			
12	Cash	$ 8,278		$ 921,249
13	Accounts receivable	42,780		331,611
14	Inventory	6,365		30,269
15	Prepaid insurance	150		450
16	Prepaid web service	200		50
17	Prepaid rent	1,800		1,800
18	Total current assets	59,573		1,285,429
19	Land	0		7,500
20	Building, net	0		67,110
21	Equipment, net	3,600		101,715
22	Van, net	27,245		110,970
23	Total assets	$ 90,418		$ 1,572,724

	A	B	C	D
24				
25	**Liabilites**			
26	Accounts payable	$ 18,950	$	18,711
27	Current portion of notes payable	6,000		8,710
28	Other payables	2,806		4,359
29	Unearned revenues			
30	**Total current liabilities**	27,756		31,780
31	Notes payable	24,000		96,290
32	**Total liabilities**	51,756		128,070
33				
34	**Equity**			
35	Common stock	$ 5,000	$	7,500
36	Additional paid-in capital			1,247,500
37	Retained earnings	33,662		189,654
38	**Total shareholders' equity**	38,662		1,444,654
39				
40	**Total liabilities and shareholders' equity**	$ 90,418	$	1,572,724
41				

5. Beginning in column F, calculate the following ratios for Tom's Wear, Inc. for the third quarter of 2001:

   (a) Current
   (b) Acid test
   (c) Working capital
   (d) Debt to equity
   (e) Times interest earned
   (f) Return on assets
   (g) Return on equity
   (h) Gross margin percentage
   (i) Inventory turnover
   (j) Accounts receivable turnover

   All of the ratios can be calculated using your table input and formulas. Use parentheses as needed to ensure the correct calculation.

6. Beginning in column H, explain the meaning each ratio. Widen column H to 60 and wrap text as needed.

How to change page margins

7. Your spreadsheet has two distinct sections – the data input (income and balance sheet data) and the analysis. In order to have useable, readable printouts, the sections need to be printed separately. In order to ensure that all the data input section will print on one page, change the top and bottom page margins to 0.5 by selecting **File, Page Setup, Margins** from the menu bar. Click on the **Center on Page Horizontally** box to center the output.

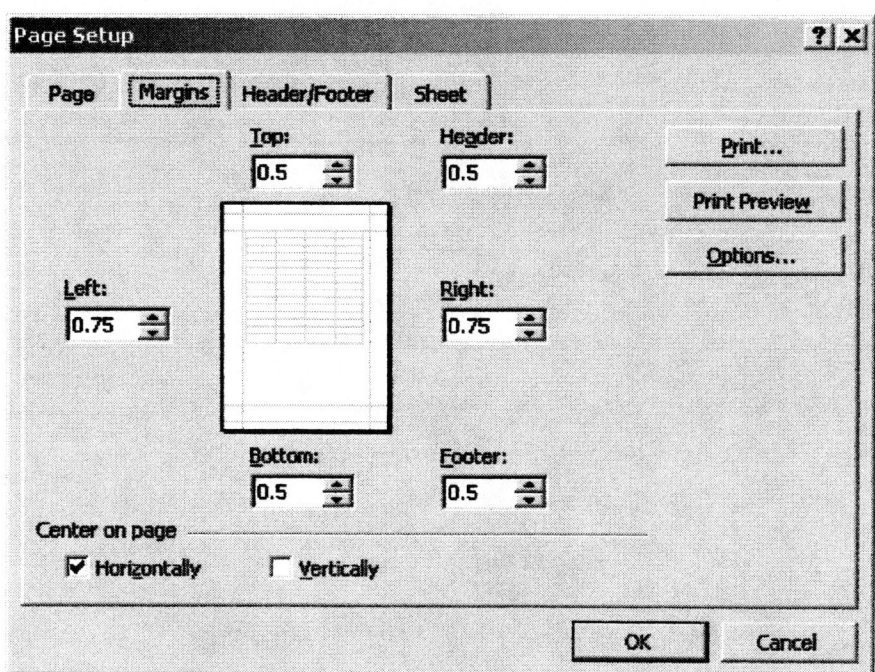

**How to print
selected areas
of your
spreadsheet**

8. Print the data input section by highlighting cells A1 to A40. The select **File, Print, Selection, OK**

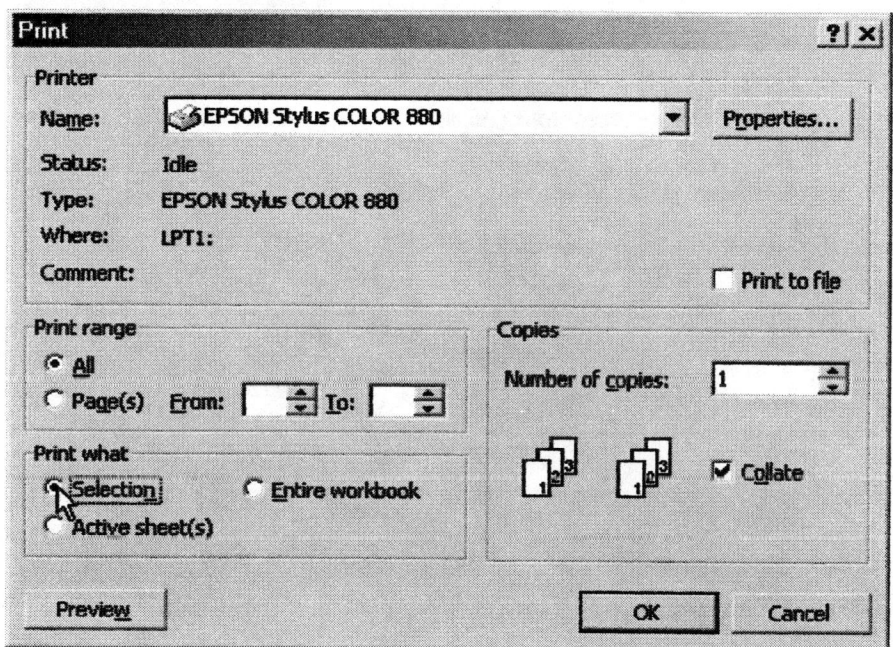

9. Improve the appearance of the analysis section by vertical centering and bordering the information in columns F – H. To center select **Format, Cells, Vertical, Center.**

How to vertically center data

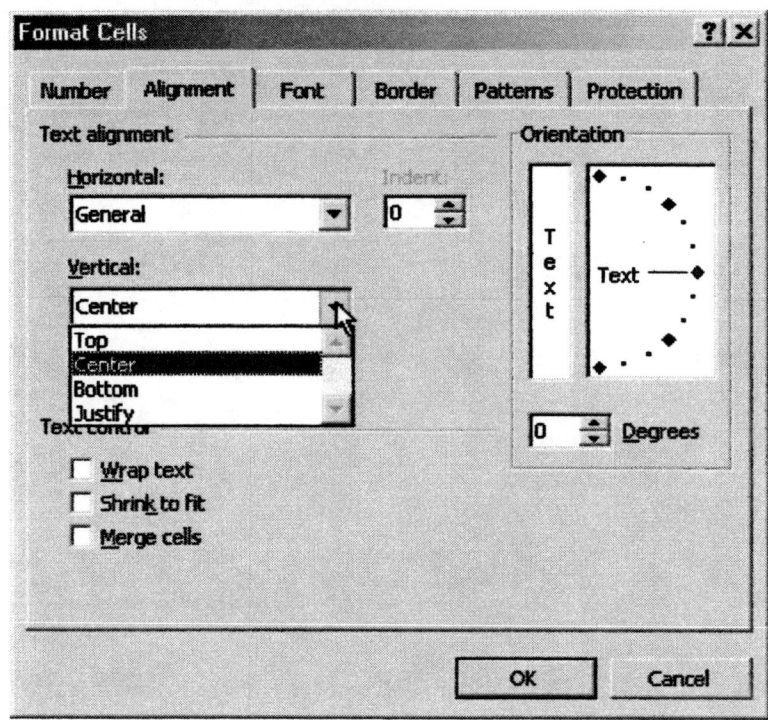

10. Print your 3rd quarter analysis by highlighting the appropriate cells and using **File, Print, Selection.**

11. Your completed analysis section should look like this (only the first five ratios are shown):

F	G	H
3rd quarter analysis		
Current ratio	40.45	Current Assets/ Current Liabilities: This ratio measures a company's ability to pay its current obligations. It is high due to the large inflow of cash from the stock offering, along with low current liabilities
Acid-test	39.42	Quick Assets / Current Liabilities: Similar to the current ratio - Tom's current assets are highly liquid.
Working capital	$ 1,253,649	Current Assets - Current Liabilities: This is almost certainly more working capital than Tom needs. The number would be expected to decrease in the coming quarters as Tom invests the funds raised from the stock offering.
Debt to equity	0.09	Total debt / Total equity: This ratio is a comparison to a company's debt to its owner financing. Most of Tom's financing is from equity.
Times interest earned	70.55	(Net income + Interest expense) / Interest expense: This ratio compares earnings to interest obligations. Tom has no problem meeting his interest obligations.

Save your spreadsheet

12. Save your file to disk by clicking the Save button . Name your file TomsWear11.

Close Excel

13. Close Excel by selecting **File, Exit** from the menu bar.

Excel Appendix

Part A
An Introduction to Computers and Excel

Accounting procedures are essentially the same whether they are performed manually or on a computer.

Excel is a computerized worksheet or spreadsheet that can be used by accountants to help analyze numbers and data. Each worksheet consists of columns and rows. Thus, Excel may be considered a computerized ledger. Although you can add text to an Excel worksheet, its main purpose is to organize numeric data. It is useful for many accounting and accounting related tasks.

In addition, computerized spreadsheets can perform accounting procedures at greater speeds and with greater accuracy than can be achieved manually. Excel can do everything your calculator can do and more. You can use Excel for very basic calculations such as adding a column of numbers or for very complex mathematical formulas. When used correctly, Excel will automatically recalculate results whenever a number is changed. It is important to recognize, however, that the computer is only a tool that can accept and process information supplied by the accountant. Each piece of data must first be analyzed and input correctly; otherwise, the worksheets generated by the computerized worksheet will contain errors and will not be useful to the business.

Before a business can begin to use a computerized worksheet, and specifically Excel, it must have the following items in place:

1. A computer system
2. Computer software
    a. Operating system software
    b. Microsoft Excel

COMPUTER SYSTEM

A computer system consists of several electronic components that together have the ability to accept user-supplied data; input, store, and execute programmed instructions; and output results according to use specifications. The physical computer and its related devices are the hardware, while the stored program that supplies the instructions is called the software.

To understand how a computer system works, we must first look at a conceptual computer that demonstrates the major components and functions of a computer system. The conceptual computer shown in Figure A-1 has four major elements — input devices, processing/internal memory unit, secondary storage devices, and output devices. The illustration also shows the flow of data into the computer and the flow of processed information out of the computer.

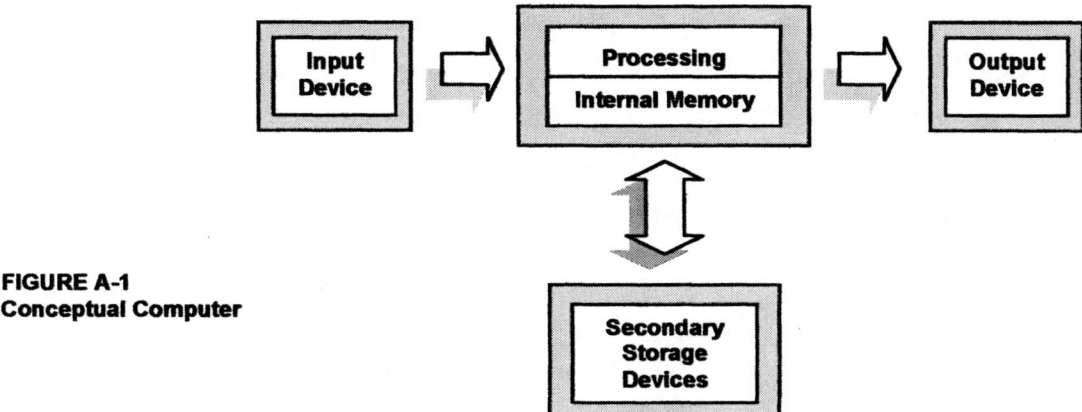

FIGURE A-1
Conceptual Computer

Input devices are used to feed data and instructions into the computer. Once the data and instructions are entered, the computer must be able to store them internally and then process the data based on the instructions. Storage and processing occur in the processing/internal memory unit.

There are two types of internal computer memory: random-access memory (RAM) and read-only memory (ROM). RAM is the largest portion of the memory but still has limited capacity; consequently, secondary storage devices are needed. In addition, RAM is temporary—anything stored in RAM is erased when power to the computer is interrupted. Therefore, data stored in RAM must be saved to a secondary storage medium through the use of a secondary storage device before the power is turned off. ROM is permanent memory and consists of those instruction sets necessary to start the computer and receive initial messages from input devices. ROM takes up only a small portion of the total internal memory capacity of a computer system.

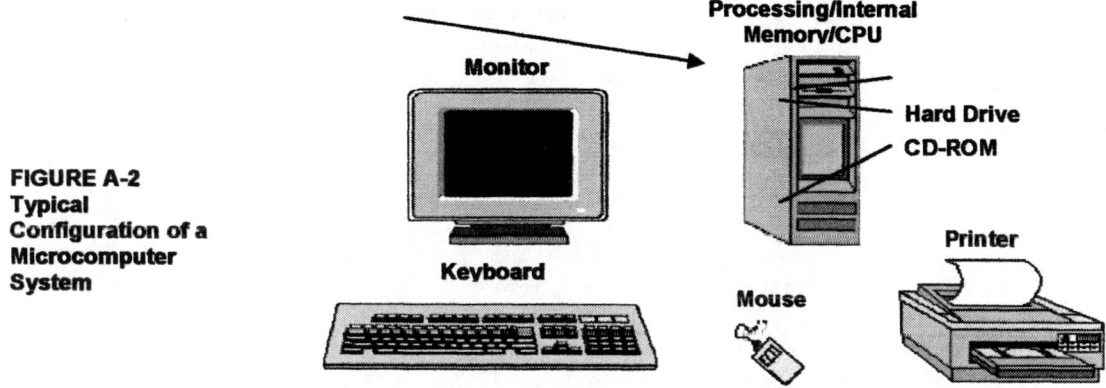

FIGURE A-2
Typical
Configuration of a
Microcomputer
System

Finally, the results of processing must be made available to computer users through output devices. These components form a collection of devices referred to as computer hardware because they have physical substance. In a typical microcomputer system (see Figure A-2), a keyboard and mouse are used for input and a printer and monitor are used for output. The processing/internal memory unit is housed inside a box along with secondary storage devices consisting of a hard drive unit, one or more floppy disk drives, and a CD-ROM drive.

Computer hardware can do nothing without a computer program. Computer programs are supplied on floppy disks or CD-ROMs, which are secondary storage media used in floppy disk or CD-ROM drives. Figure A-3 shows an example of a floppy disk and of a CD-ROM.

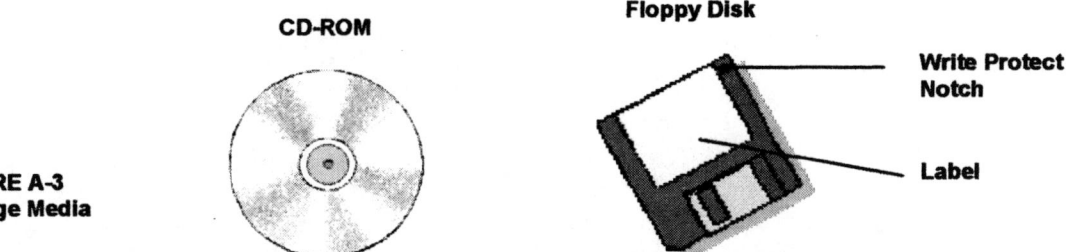

CD-ROM　　　　　**Floppy Disk**

Write Protect Notch

Label

**FIGURE A-3
Storage Media**

To operate a particular computer program you must first load the program into the system's internal memory (RAM) through the use of a floppy disk or CD-ROM drive or by accessing the program that has been installed and stored on the system's hard drive. Once RAM accesses a program, the computer can execute the program instructions and process data as directed by the user through the keyboard or mouse. At the end of a processing session, the results may be viewed on the monitor, printed on the printer, and/or stored permanently on a floppy disk or hard drive.

COMPUTER SOFTWARE

The computer can do nothing without a computer program. Computer programs control the input, processing, storage, and output operations of a computer. Computer programmers write the instructions that tell the computer to execute certain procedures and process data. There are two broad categories of computer software; operating system software and applications software.

Operating System Software

Operating system software links the computer hardware, the applications software, and the computer user. It consists of programs that start up the computer, retrieve applications programs, and allow the computer operator to store and retrieve data. Operating system software controls access to input and output devices and access to applications programs. There are several popular operating systems for microcomputers. They include Windows 95/98/2000, DOS, DOS combined with Windows 3.XX, OS/2, the Macintosh operating system, and UNIX.

Applications Software

Applications software refers to programs designed for a specific use. The five most common types of business applications software are database management, spreadsheet, word processing, communications, and graphics. Spreadsheet software allows the manipulation of data and has the ability to project answers to "what if" questions. For example, a spreadsheet program could project a company's profit next year if sales increased by 10 percent and expenses increased by six percent. Word processing software enables the user to write and print letters, memos, and other documents. Graphic software displays data visually in the form of graphic images. Communications software allows your computer to "talk" to other computers, but to accomplish communications you need additional hardware: a modem to transmit and receive data over telephone lines. Database management software stores, retrieves, sorts, and updates an organized body of information. Most computerized accounting systems are designed as database management software. Accounting information is data that must be organized and stored in a common base of data. This allows the entry of data and the retrieval of information in an organized and systematic way.

Applications software is frequently linked with a particular operating system. Database management, spreadsheet, word processing, graphics, communication, accounting, and other software applications are available in versions that work with most of the popular operating systems. For example, if your computer system is using Windows 98, you would purchase the Windows 98 version of a word processing program. If you were using a Macintosh computer and operating system you would purchase the Macintosh version of a spreadsheet program.

Accounting Applications Software   Most computerized accounting software is organized into modules. Each module is designed to process a particular type of accounting data such as accounts receivable, accounts payable, or payroll. Each module is also designed to work in conjunction with the other modules. When modules are designed to work together in this manner, they are referred to as integrated software. In an integrated accounting system each module handles a different function but also communicates with the other modules. For example, to record a sale on account, you would make an entry into the accounts receivable module. The integration feature automatically records this entry in the sales journal, updates the customer's account in the accounts receivable subsidiary ledger, and posts all accounts affected in the general ledger. Thus in an integrated accounting system, transaction data are only entered once. All of the other accounting procedures required to bring the accounting records up-to-date are performed automatically through the integration function.

Microsoft Excel   Excel has been selected as the computerized spreadsheet program for this book. It is easy to use, fully integrated, and is also available in versions that work with several different operating systems. The assignments contained in this text are designed to illustrate how spreadsheets can be used to analyze and present accounting data. They are not intended to provide a comprehensive course of study for a computerized spreadsheet.

WORKING WITH EXCEL

Before you begin to work with Excel you need to be familiar with your computer hardware and the Windows operating system. When you are running Windows, your work takes place on the desktop. Think of this area as resembling the surface of a desk. There are physical objects on your real desk and there are windows and icons on the Windows desktop. There are minor differences between the various versions of Windows. The figures here will reflect a typical Windows 98 Desktop. Other Windows versions will have small differences but will be fundamentally the same.

A mouse is an essential input device for all Windows applications. A mouse is a pointing device that assumes different shapes on your monitor as you move the mouse on your desk. According to the nature of the current action, the mouse pointer may appear as a small arrowhead, an hourglass, or a hand. There are five basic mouse techniques:

◆	Click	To quickly press and release the left mouse button.
◆	Double-click	To click the left mouse button twice in rapid succession.
◆	Drag	To hold down the left mouse button while you move the mouse.
◆	Point	To position the mouse pointer over an object without clicking a button.
◆	Right-click	To quickly press and release the right mouse button.

The Windows 98 Desktop

Figure A-4 shows a typical opening Windows 98 screen. Your desktop may be different, just as your real desk is arranged differently from those of your colleagues.

◆ **Desktop icons:** Graphic representations of drives, files, and other resources. The desktop icons that display will vary depending on your computer setup.

◆ **Start button:** Clicking on the Start button displays the start menu and lets you start applications.

◆ **Taskbar:** Contains the start button and other buttons representing open applications.

FIGURE A-4 Windows 98 Desktop (Partial)

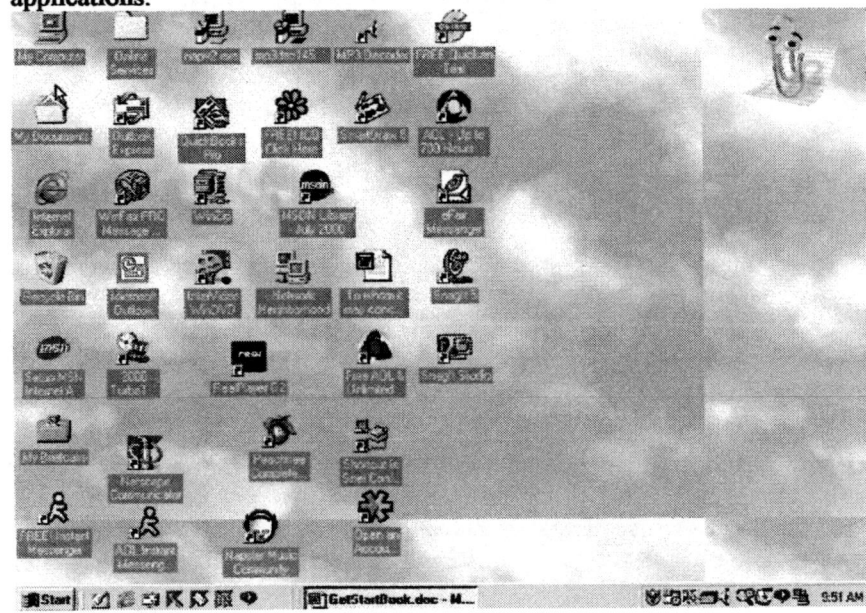

Applications Window

The Excel program window starts out as a blank worksheet. (Your blank worksheet may look slightly different, depending upon the version of Excel you are using.) Regardless of the windows that are open on your desktop, most windows have certain elements in common.

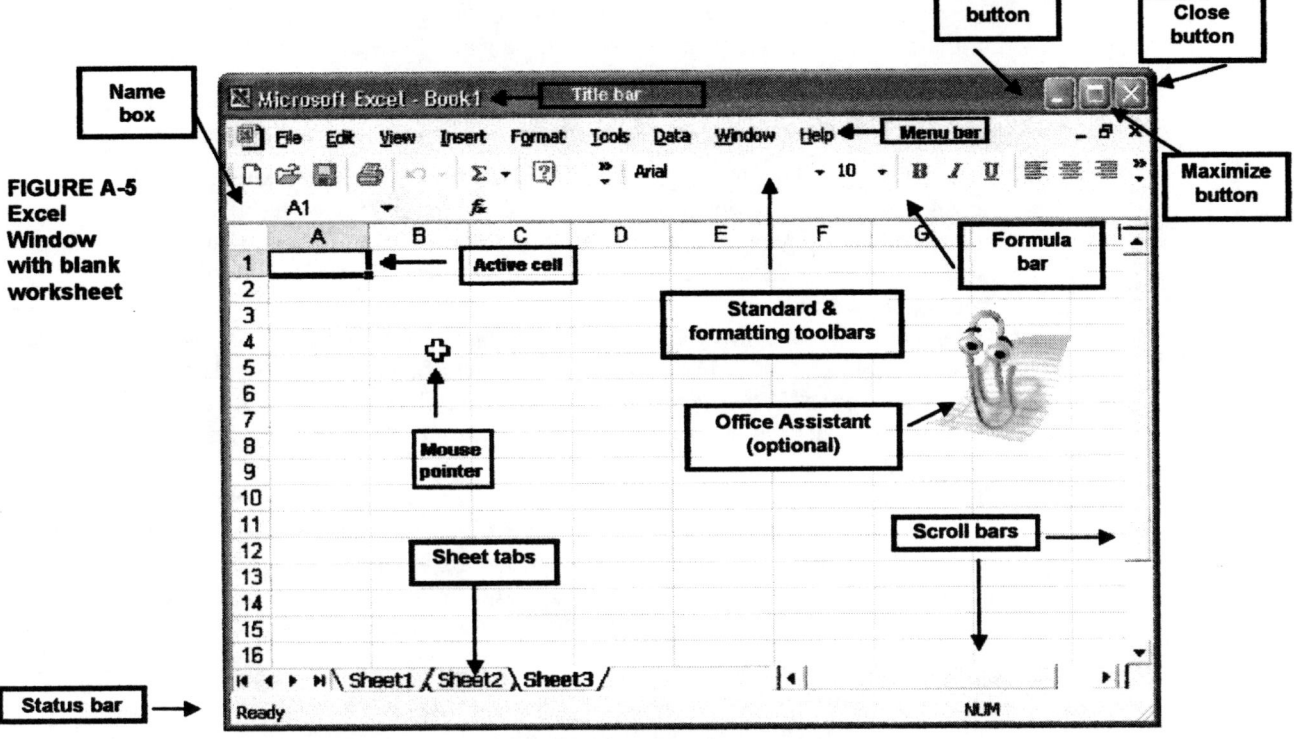

FIGURE A-5
Excel
Window
with blank
worksheet

♦ **Minimize button:** Clicking on this button minimizes a window and displays it as a task button on the taskbar.

♦ **Maximize button:** Clicking on this button enlarges the window so that it fills the entire desktop. After you enlarge a window, the maximize button is replaced by a Restore button (a double box, not shown) that returns the window to the size it was before it was maximized.

♦ **Close button:** Clicking on this button will close the window.

♦ **Title bar:** Displays the name of the application. In Excel, the title bar also contains the file name. The default file name when you start Excel is Book 1.

♦ **Menu bar:** This window element lists the available menus for the window.

♦ **Status bar:** A line of text at the bottom of many windows that gives more information about a field. If you are unsure of what to enter in a field, select it with your mouse and read the status bar.

Other main components of the Excel window include:

♦ **Toolbars:** Excel has a variety of toolbars available that organize and allow access to various Excel commands. The defaults are the **Standard** and **Formatting** toolbars. The Standard toolbar buttons correspond to Excel's most used commands. The Formatting toolbar buttons are the most common ones used to change a worksheet's appearance.

♦ **Active cell:** An Excel worksheet consists of cells. Cells are the rectangles where rows and columns intersect. Each cell can have one entry – text or numeric. The active cell is the cell you are currently working on. It is identified by a dark border. Cells are referenced by their column and row. For example, in the illustration above, the active cell is A1. The cell reference for the active cell is shown in the name box. You can change the active cell using either the keyboard or the mouse.

♦ **Formula bar:** This displays the active cell's contents – text, number or formula.

♦ **Mouse pointer:** This moves on the screen as a user moves the mouse.

♦ **Scroll bars:** These allow you to move to other areas of a worksheet using the mouse. When you click on the arrows on one of the bars, you move in the direction of the arrow. You may also move to other areas of a worksheet by dragging a scroll bar.

♦ **Sheet tabs:** Excel allows you to save multiple worksheets in one file, if desired. Each worksheet has a sheet tab that identifies its name. The defaults are shown above. When you open a new file in Excel, the default is three worksheets. Clicking a sheet tab allows you to change to a different worksheet.

♦ **Office Assistant:** This is an optional feature available in Excel and other Microsoft Office applications. It is designed to assist you in accessing the built-in help files. When you click on the office assistant (left mouse button), he allows you to ask a question. Right-clicking the office assistant allows you to change options, change the appearance or hide the office assistant.

Using Menus

Commands are listed on menus, as shown in Figure A-6. Each item on the **Main Menu Bar** has its own menus, which are listed by selecting the menu. When a menu is displayed, choose a command by clicking on it or by typing the **Underlined letter** to execute the command. You can also bypass the menu entirely if you know the **Keyboard equivalent** shown to the right of the command when the menu is displayed.

A **Dimmed command** indicates that a command is not currently executable; some additional action has to be taken for the command to become available. Some commands are followed by **arrows** indicating a submenu exists. Double arrows pointing downward at the bottom of a menu indicate that more menu options exist. The other options are accessible by clicking the double arrows.

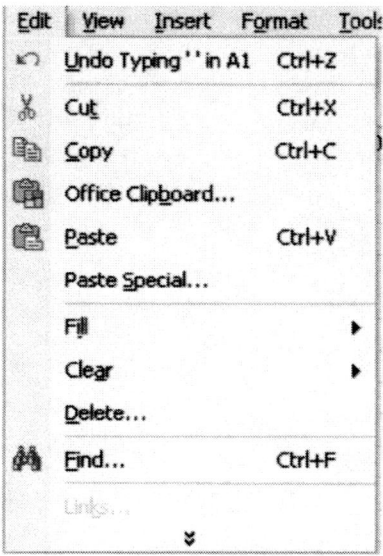

Working in the Windows 98 Environment

You can use a combination of mouse and keyboard techniques to navigate within the Windows 98 environment. For example, you can click on an item to select it, and then press the ENTER key to choose it, or you can just double-click on the item. Excel is designed for a mouse, but it also provides keyboard equivalents for almost every command. It may seem confusing at first that there are several different ways to do the same thing. You will find this flexibility useful. For example, if your hands are already on the keyboard, it may be faster to use the keyboard equivalent of a mouse command. Alternatively, if your hand is already on the mouse, it may be faster to use the mouse technique to carry out a command. When a procedure in an assignment says to select or choose an item, generally use whichever method you prefer. Alternative procedures are often provided as well. It is not necessary to memorize any particular technique, just be flexible and willing to experiment. As you gain experience with the program, you will develop personal preferences, and the various techniques will become second nature.

Opening a File in Excel

As with any other Windows program, files in Excel are opened from the **File** menu. When you enter the program, select **File, New** to open a blank workbook or **File Open** to open an existing file. The last four files saved in Excel appear at the bottom of the **File** menu. Those files may be accessed simply by clicking on their name.

Saving a File in Excel

You should save your files frequently to prevent loss of work. Files can be saved by clicking the **Save Button** 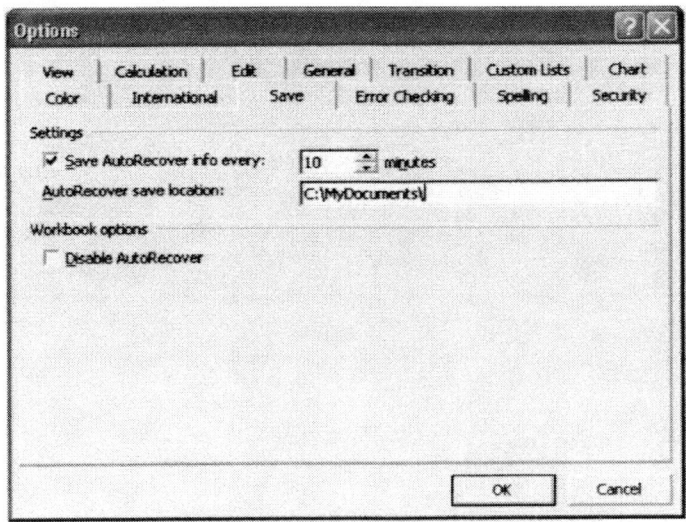 or by choosing Save or Save As… off the **File Menu**. To set up automatically saving of files select the **Tools** menu, click **Options**, and then click the **Save** tab. Select the **Save AutoRecover info every** check box. Specify how often you want Microsoft Excel to save files in the minute box. **AutoRecover should not be used as substitute for regularly saving your work.**

PART B
Installing Excel

This section of the appendix discusses several basic operations that you need to complete to install Excel for use in completing the computer Workshop assignments in this text.

SYSTEM REQUIREMENTS

The recommended minimum software and hardware requirements your computer system needs to run both Windows and Microsoft Excel successfully are:

◆ Microsoft Excel

◆ Microsoft Window 95 or higher, or Windows NT 4.0 or higher.

◆ A personal computer with a Pentium II 233 MHz or higher processor.

◆ A hard disk with a minimum of 60 MB of free disk space (100 MB recommended) and a CD-ROM drive.

◆ An additional 40 MB of free disk space during installation.

◆ One 3.5 inch high-density floppy disk drive (if student floppy backups are desired).

◆ At least 32 MG of RAM minimum (64 MB recommended).

◆ A 256 color SVGA, or similar high-resolution monitor that is supported by Windows.

◆ A printer that is supported by Windows, if you want to print your solutions.

◆ A mouse that is supported by Windows.

Using Excel on a Network

Excel can be used in a network environment as long as each student uses a separate source to store his or her data files. Students should consult with their instructor and/or network administrator for specific procedures regarding program installation and any special printing procedures required for proper network operation.

PART C
Correcting Mistakes

When typing information in a cell, you may correct mistakes by pressing the Backspace key. Each time you press backspace, a character is deleted from your input. Pressing the Esc key cancels all changes and puts the cell back to its original contents. To change information already entered into a cell, make the cell active and press the F2 key to edit the information or simply click your mouse in the formula bar to edit its contents.